I0435206

HOW TO RATE YOUR LOCAL POLICE

A User's Guide for Civic Leaders, Governmental
Officials, Concerned Citizens, and Police

Chief David C. Couper

For all the men and women in blue with whom I was privileged work and lead.

"Closer to the people we serve!"

Burnsville, Minn.
Madison, Wisc.

CONTENTS

INTRODUCTION

A number of years ago, after a discussion with Gary Hayes who was the director of the newly-formed Police Executive Research Forum in Washington, D.C., I was moved to write a short monograph on how to rate police. In it, I would explain to civic leaders, governmental officials, and police what a "good" police department was and how it could be measured.

Many years have passed since that exciting and innovative time when police were seriously discussing how to improve, get closer to those whom they served, and solve community-identified problems.[1]

Today, there is a national discussion regarding the use of deadly force by police and the growing mistrust of police among people of color. This is a serious matter and must be addressed. For without trust and support, the effectiveness of police officers in a free society is severely compromised.

While I have long retired from active policing, my interest in the men and women who serve as our police remains extremely high. Since 2011, I have maintained an active blog to address the areas I feel are necessary to

---

[1] *Problem-Oriented Policing*, Herman Goldstein, McGraw-Hill, 1990.

improve police: leadership, handling of protest, control in the use of force, a deeper and sustained community-orientation, and higher standards for the recruitment, selection, and training of our police.[2]

In 2012, after five years of work, I published a book that described my career as a transformative chief of police, a history of long-term organizational change in the police department in Madison, Wisc., and specific steps that must be taken if our nation's police are to improve.[3]

I invite you to use this monograph as a way to evaluate police in your community. If you find them acting consistent with the guiding principles presented, let them know, give them your support, and help them continue on the road to excellence; to continuously improve all that they do.

If, on the other hand, you find areas in which your local police are deficient, call this to their attention and offer to help them improve.

A great nation such as ours deserves a great police.

---

[2] http://improvingpolice.wordpress.com.

[3] *Arrested Development: A Veteran Police Chief Sounds Off About Protest, Racism, Corruption and the Seven Steps Necessary to Improve Our Nation's Police*, David C. Couper, CreateSpace, 2012.

1

MYTHS ABOUT POLICE

- *Low crime rates show that a police agency is efficient and effective.*
- *A high arrest rate shows that the police are doing a good job.*
- *A high rate of police officers to citizens means high quality police service.*
- *Responding quickly to citizens' calls for services show that a police agency is effective.*

These are a few of the standards by which the public judges the quality of a police agency. But none of these standards provides an accurate measure of how good or bad a police agency is: none of them can tell us how effectively a police agency is dealing with problems of public safety and order. How then, can we tell a good police agency from a bad one? What kinds of things should we be looking for?

To find the elusive and difficult answers to these questions, we must first develop an understanding of the complexity of police work in modern society. The police are asked to fulfill many complicated and interrelated roles, each involving a variety of functions and tasks. They must control crime, maintain order, render aid and provide emergency services, 24 hours a day, seven days a week, to all the areas of the communities they serve. Measuring how well the police are performing these tasks requires clear and specific definitions of the agency's goals and objectives. Unfortunately, these goals can be ambiguous, and often are subject to a variety of interpretations.

For example, does controlling crime mean vigorously enforcing all the traffic laws and pursuing all types of illegal gambling? In some situations, goals can conflict: in a public protest, for instance, is maintaining order more important than arresting those who are in the thoroughfare blocking the flow of traffic? Objectives can vary in meaning from one community to another and even, in some communities, from one neighborhood to another. Are the kinds of behavior and activity permitted in the downtown business district acceptable in the suburban neighborhood? Add to these questions the problems of setting priorities and allocating resources to accomplish these goals. Without a clear and generally agreed-upon idea of what the police should be doing, it is difficult to rate how well they are doing it.

Rating the police is further complicated by unrealistic expectations of what the police can do. Each citizen expects the police to meet many goals, according to his or her own value system and an understanding of what their police can and should do. For instance, one person may expect an officer should be sent to personally take their report of a crime, regardless of its seriousness or likelihood of solution. Another person would be satisfied if their report of a minor theft were simply taken over the telephone and a police case number given to them for insurance purposes. Again, some citizens may desire police walk foot patrols in their neighborhoods, while others would prefer officers to patrol in motor vehicles. The expectations of citizens are often unrealistic and contradictory and the police cannot begin to satisfy all of them. Having said that, there must always be opportunities for frequent contact and dialogue about expectations between community members and their police.

Uncertain objectives and unrealistic expectations cause people to rate police agencies in hazy and unspecific terms, largely because they cannot get accurate information with which to judge agency performance. Because many agencies are shrouded in secrecy, and make little effort to be more transparent, there is no way to assess their procedures or how well their officers are performing. Nor can citizens know without great difficulty how police are selected, trained and deployed. Nor is there information available about what officers actually do to maintain order, investigate crimes, and provide other services -- two of the three main functions of police.

Moreover, the more extensive information on crime control can produce inaccuracy and distortion if citizens try to compare one jurisdiction's crime rates with those of another. This is because of the variations in social and economic conditions among communities and, unfortunately, practice among some in police leadership to underreport crime in their jurisdictions.

Lacking the information they need to make rational judgments, people (including their elected representatives), rate police on the basis of their own perceptions of what they should do, or they tend to use crime occurrences, arrests, and clearance rates, the data police make available to them, as measures of police effectiveness. Those measures, in turn, give rise to a number of myths about what makes a good police agency. In the following section, we will try to dispel some of those myths.

Myth #1: Low crime rates show that a police agency is efficient and effective.

To the three basic objectives of the police -- controlling crime, maintaining order and providing services -- we have to add the basic and justifiable expectation that the police should make citizens feel secure in their community. This expectation, influenced by the public's perception of crime, or the police ability to control crime, must be realistic if the police are to be measured by how well they contribute to this sense of safety. Many people believe that police are solely responsible for reducing crime and, accordingly, that an effective police agency will necessarily insure a low reported crime rate.

But research has shown that social and economic factors have an enormous influence on the nature and levels of reported crime in a particular community. In fact, the FBI's annual *Uniform Crime Report,* which establishes the framework for collecting and analyzing each community's crime statistics, lists the following factors as having the greatest influence on crime:

1. The size of the community and its population, how crowded the area is;
2. The make up of the population, particularly in terms of age structure;
3. Stability of the population with respect to residence, mobility, and transience;
4. Economic conditions, including job availability;
5. Cultural conditions, such as educational, recreational, and religious characteristics;
6. Climate;
7. Effective strength of law enforcement agencies;
8. What law enforcement emphasizes in its administrative and investigative roles;
9. The policies of other components of the criminal

justice system (i.e., prosecutorial, judicial, correctional, and probational);
10. Citizens' attitudes toward crime; and
11. How citizens report crime.

Because police cannot control these socio-economic factors, they should not be held responsible for all increases or decreases in crime. This doesn't mean that police play no role in controlling crime. In fact, they do play a major role in controlling street crimes, such as purse snatching and muggings. But police cannot fairly be held accountable for all crime such as crimes of passion committed among relatives or friends or crimes committed indoors, such as retail theft and most white collar crimes. Police should actively collaborate with those who work in other systems which have an impact on crime, such as public education, job creation, employment opportunities, prosecution, adjudication and correctional systems, and community recreational programs.

Crime rates are determined primarily by citizen reporting rates, which vary from neighborhood to neighborhood and from city to city. Studies show that crimes reported to the police represent only a portion of the crime that actually occurs, and that people decide not to report many crimes, either because they think the police can't do anything to solve them, they want to avoid having to deal with the cumbersome and lethargic criminal justice system, or simply because they do not trust police or our system of justice.

The irony is that, because people who live in a community where the police agency is responsive and trusted are more likely to report crimes than those who view the police as adversaries. In these communities, police will receive more reports of crime simply because citizens are more confident in the ability of the police to respond appropriately and effectively. The result is that a community with a very good police agency will often have a high crime reporting rate. Conversely, a poor police agency will often have a low rate of crime reporting by its community.

The questionable methods by which crime rates are determined is another reason why they are limited in measuring the quality of a police agency. For instance, only the following serious crimes are included in the official crime rate -- homicide, aggravated assault, robbery, rape, burglary, larceny, auto theft, and arson. Other criminal activity, such as drug and weapons offenses, is not considered. Moreover, the crime rate is computed by dividing the total number of reported crimes by population increments of 100,000. This procedure dilutes the meaning of the measure because four of the crimes -- burglary, auto theft, larceny and arson -- are directed at motor vehicles, structures (stores and homes), and objects, not people. Furthermore, the rate for these property crimes often fluctuates according to the availability of new targets such as high-rise apartment buildings, high-end bicycles, or the latest smart phone version. Rape, on the other hand, because it predominately affects women, should not be computed against the community's entire population.

These problems in compiling crime rates, the solution of which the police in most cases cannot prevent or solve, make the measure very inaccurate as an indication of how well police are performing.

Are there better ways to measure crime? The National Crime Victimization Survey (NCVS) is a much better method and could be modified to include governmental jurisdictions like the UCR does.[4]

---

[4] See http://www.bjs.gov/index.cfm?ty=dcdetail&iid=245.

Myth #2: A high arrest rate shows that the police are doing a good job.

Arrest statistics, or the number of arrests made by the police, are misleading because many arrests are made for reasons other than to prosecute a criminal. The arrest of a person, putting them into jail, is not a police goal in and of itself. The power of arrest is used as a means to achieve the three basic objectives: controlling crime, maintaining order, and providing services (all, of course, within the rule of law). Sometimes the police use their arrest power to control a known criminal; or to provide the basis for further investigation; or to help the sick, as in taking into protective custody a person without shelter; or to manage a mentally ill person causing a disturbance; or to take a range of other custodial actions which give police authority to deal with a problem (i.e., laws which exist today permitting police to take inebriated persons to a detoxification center or disturbed persons in danger of harming themselves or others to a mental health facility).

Other factors, beyond the control of the police, govern many arrests and make arrest statistics misleading. For example, did the victim report the crime right away? Did he or she describe or identify the suspect? Were there witnesses, and are they willing to come forward? Is there any evidence, and is it of good quality? These factors depend most directly on the responses of the victim, but they also include the criminal's skill in eluding police detection. Moreover, if the police do make an arrest, it could be a "bad" arrest -- that is, one that the prosecutor might dismiss for lack of evidence or because police violated the suspect's right to due process. On the other hand, the arrest may be "good," but the prosecutor may dismiss it because of a lack of interest in pursuing that type of case, or as a means of reducing a heavy caseload.

To use arrest statistics as a yardstick for measuring the quality of a police agency is misleading because those statistics look at only one aspect of police work -- albeit an important one -- crime control. Even so, the police do a great deal more to control crime than just arrest a suspect after a crime has occurred. Police work involves crime prevention efforts, deterrence activities, and gathering information about patterns of crime. Since arrest statistics do not include these aspects of crime control -- much less the order maintenance and service aspects of police work-- their usefulness as a measure of police agency quality is limited.

Related to arrest statistics are clearance rates, the number of cases resolved by either the arrest of a suspect or by "exceptional" means. Exceptional means include the death or suicide of a suspect or a suspect's confession to crimes in addition to the one that caused the arrest. In either case, the clearance of a particular crime means the police have closed their investigation of it. Like arrest rates, clearance rates are open to question as a valid indication of police quality. Some agencies, for instance, inflate their clearance rates by loosely interpreting the criteria for clearance or by getting suspects to admit to committing other crimes in exchange for lighter charges in the pending case.

Each of these measures -- crime, arrest, and clearance rates -- is imperfect and unreliable as a single measure of effectiveness, but that does not mean they are entirely useless. Crime rates for the crimes the police can affect, such as street muggings, when looked at within one jurisdiction over a period of several years, with no changes in reporting procedures, can shed some light on police effectiveness. Likewise arrest and clearance rates, over several-year periods and for particular kinds of crime, can be helpful in assessing police patrol and investigation operations. For example, the number of arrests in murder cases is unimportant if, in a good number of the cases, the murderer turns himself in or is readily apparent. But if the cases require investigation to identify and prosecute the murderer, the number of arrests or clearances is significant. For any crime in which some police activity or effort could lead to an arrest, arrest and clearance rates are important.

What citizens need to remember is that none of these measures, taken alone, can give an accurate picture of a police agency's effectiveness. Crime, arrest, and clearance rates, when broken down into greater detail and knowledgeably analyzed, can provide some insights into how well the police are controlling crime.

Myth #3: A high ratio of police officers to citizens means high quality police services.

Nothing could be farther from the truth. This measure ignores the diversity among communities' social-economic structures, their use of public services, the nature of their crime problems, and the expectations that a community has of its police agency. Shoplifting in Beverly Hills and ski larcenies in Aspen require dramatically different police responses than arson in the South Bronx or narcotics trafficking in Miami. Communities where the police answer medical emergencies, act as school crossing guards, or simply run errands for local government officials, require different numbers of police officers from communities where these tasks are not required or are handled by other agencies. Use of this police-citizen ratio as a measure of quality is based on the erroneous assumption that having more officers will result in lower reported crime rates when, in fact, the opposite may occur. More police officers on the streets could increase citizen's confidence in the ability of police to solve crimes and, accordingly, their willingness to report crimes to the police. Thus, the number of police officers a community employs in relation to its population is seldom a measure of agency quality. It is used primarily by people who are more interested in expanding or reducing the number of officers in a community than in determining the quality of police services.

Myth #4: Responding quickly to citizen's calls for services shows that a police agency is efficient.

How quickly a police officer arrives to answer citizen's calls for police service, termed "response time," has, from time to time, been viewed as a valid measure of an effective police agency. An agency whose response time to all its calls is faster than it was in previous years, or faster than another police agency's, or simply faster than some mythical average, is considered to be providing excellent police service. Many people assume that the more rapidly the police respond to calls about crimes, the more likely they are to catch and arrest the suspect. But the fact is, because crime victims and witnesses usually wait five or ten minutes before they call the police, rapid response rarely leads to an arrest.

In fact, police receive many more routine calls for service than calls about crimes. Sometimes the incident is an emergency, such as a prowler in the back yard or an injured child, in which the caller expects and deserves immediate attention. Other calls, such as report of a stolen bicycle taken during the evening hours or a continuing landlord-tenant dispute, do not require, nor should the caller expect, an immediate response. Sending a police unit immediately to every call for police service is not only unnecessary, but also a tremendous drain on police resources.

A carefully developed range of responses based on the seriousness of the call, when the incident occurred, and the needs of the caller would provide the most effective police response. This kind of system would allow the police to respond quickly to serious calls requiring immediate police presence. Because of the variable nature of police calls for service and the differences in appropriate kinds of police response, overall response time cannot be used as a single measure of police effectiveness.

2

RATING YOUR POLICE

The traditional methods -- the crime rate, the number of arrests, the clearance rate, the ratio of officers to citizens, and response time -- used to measure a police agency's overall quality and effectiveness are very limited. They cannot tell you if you have a good police agency. Instead, you need to ask questions about the leadership, policies, and organizational characteristics of your police agency. Only when you understand the answers to these questions will the traditional statistical measures, when used cautiously and in conjunction with the characteristics of a police agency, have any meaning for rating your police.

One of the reasons for this publication is to frame some essential questions to help you think about what these characteristics might be. Citizens are currently asking the wrong questions about their police. Personal measures of satisfaction are deficient as measures for rating a police agency because personal satisfaction may be achieved at the expense of larger community interests. Nevertheless, sound random surveying, using what the business sector has learned about customer satisfaction, can be informative and reveal citizen attitudes regarding how they perceive police; especially in matters of trust and respect. Until citizens begin to ask the right questions, they will never be able to rate their police intelligently and realistically.

The questions asked in the following sections are based on general considerations, keeping in mind broader knowledge of policing and larger, community-wide interests. As important as they are, the three sets of questions are secondary to the primary, essential question:

- **Is your police agency fair and effective in fulfilling its responsibilities to you and your community?**

3

LEADERSHIP CHARACTERISTICS

What kind of person is the chief?

The police chief should be a visible and accessible leader who thoughtfully strives to improve the effectiveness of police services. The leadership ability of the chief is the single most important ingredient in a good police agency. Police agencies, like all large bureaucracies, tend to resist change. Improvements can be made only if the person at the top is willing to challenge the *status quo,* take risks, be innovative, and build a coalition of support for change. Improvements are not automatic with a committed police chief, but they are impossible without one. Change for the sake of change is wasteful and inefficient. But because all police agencies need to constantly monitor the fairness and effectiveness of their services, a willingness to change, to continuously improve, is an essential characteristic for all police chiefs. To make those improvements, the chief must have a clear vision of the agency's objectives, the role of police in a democratic society, and how to successfully and collaboratively achieve those objectives. Additionally, a police chief must have the vision, self-confidence, persistence, and passion to chart an improvement course and see it through.

Finally, to the list of essential characteristics for a police chief, add personal integrity, the respect of the community and elected officials, and the ability to inspire and motivate his or her officers to share the vision and work to the best of their ability.

What tone does the chief set for the agency?

The chief sets the tone for the agency through both actions and words. An aggressive tone could translate into physically and abusive officers, insensitive to citizen's rights to due process. Or the chief can emphasize restraint, requiring all officers to exercise civility at all times and to meticulously observe the legal rights of all citizens they encounter.

In a large dimension, the police chief also sets the tone in the community for discussion of all public safety and law enforcement issues. The chief must present a coherent crime control philosophy as well as concrete crime prevention strategies, striking a balance between the conflicting demands of freedom and public order, majority rule and minority rights, government authority and individual rights, and resisting the pressures from various powerful interest groups. For example, to "do something" to remove an annoying group of protesters, or "clear the streets" of poor or homeless people who are not breaking the law. A thoughtful chief must defend the right of unpopular groups to exercise their Constitutional guarantees to freedom of speech and assembly, as well as safeguard the physical safety of those who choose to exercise these rights, protect powerless, unpopular and disfranchised groups from police harassment or intimidation, and insure that all citizens, regardless of gender, class, race, ethnicity, citizenship status, or sexual orientation, receive the same respectful level of police services.

A strong, effective police chief will not hesitate to take public stands on controversial issues facing the community, balancing the legitimate law enforcement needs of the officers and the safety concerns of the community. It is the chief's responsibility to educate each group about the other's interests and perspectives. While a perfect solution to many of these conflicts is rare, the effort put forth to listen to one another is essential in a diverse and free society such as ours.

Does the chief articulate the policies and direction of the agency clearly and understandably?

If there is community resistance or disagreement over certain police practices, the chief must acknowledge these differences, discuss them in a fair and open manner, explain how the practice fits in with the overall direction of the agency, and then resolve the dispute by either modifying the practice or by clearly explaining why one course of action was chosen over another.

The chief must be able to:

- Mediate complex community problems,

- Speak out on controversial public safety issues.

- Offer citizens a coherent definition of the role of police in a democratic society.

The chief's roles are many and complex:

- Spokesperson on crime control and public safety;

- Advisor on personal security;

- Preserver of due process guarantees;

- Defender of minority rights;

- Protector of the weak, the poor, the sick, the mentally ill, and the injured;

- and

- Guardian of the rule of law and our democratic values; and

- Manager of a complex bureaucracy;

4

POLICY CHARACTERISTICS

Does the police agency have a clear sense of its objectives?

The ability of a police agency to perform its functions adequately is based upon its ability to define and understand its proper objectives, to translate these objectives into precise policies, operational procedures, and action plans, and to employ qualified professionals to carry out these objectives. While this may sound like a simple notion, it is actually very difficult. Not only is the police role complex, but it varies dramatically from community to community, depending upon the level of crime and citizens' requests for services.

A police agency must have a clear definition and vision of its overall objectives in its jurisdiction yet be able to respond to the unique requirements of particular neighborhoods. Only then will police officers know what their leaders as well as citizens expect from them. This can only be achieved by everyone working together.

At a minimum, a police agency should articulate its

role and responsibilities in the community in a written and publicly accessible mission statement and a clear articulated vision of who and what they wish to become. This can be greatly facilitated through social media, frequent public presentations, and within an agency website.

In developing a vision and mission statement, the agency should encourage community leaders, elected officials, and representatives from other criminal justice agencies to express their opinions and, perhaps, to identify enforcement priorities. The following are examples:

Mission Statement

We, the members of the police department, are committed to providing high quality police services that are accessible to all members of the community. We believe in the dignity of all people and respect individual and constitutional rights in fulfilling this mission.[5]

Vision Statement

Quality from the Inside Out.

Are there written and publicly accessible policies for all operational practices?

After developing and sharing vision and mission statements, the police agency should develop for its officers and employees a policy manual giving specific

---

[5]http://www.cityofmadison.com/police/about/mission.cfm

guidelines for achieving the mission of the agency. Although the officers should be able to exercise their professional judgment (discretion) in a range of complex situations, the manual should specify what the agency leadership expects of them, as well as what they should and should not do. Particularly in such areas as use of deadly force, search warrants, searches following an arrest, pursuit and emergency driving, stop and frisk situations, arrests, handling crowds and protests, and when SWAT teams will be used. The manual should be clear in its guidelines, and it should be subject to regular review and revision in accord with changing legal standards governing these subjects as well as new knowledge and better methods gained from research and experience.

Furthermore, the manual must define, in specific terms, examples of what constitutes illegal or improper conduct. The agency's disciplinary process should be described as clearly as possible, including safeguards for officers' rights to due process and fairness. Appeal procedures should be described for both accused officers and citizens who file complaints under these policies.

Does the police agency select the best-qualified individuals to be police officers and its leaders?

The extent to which a police agency attracts and selects a broad spectrum of qualified officers is a measure of its caliber. Officers should be chosen on the basis of their having the necessary skills, background, demeanor, and intelligence for police work, regardless of their race, gender, physical size, or sexual orientation, and without resort to such arbitrary measures as physical strength, size, or bravado. Selection criteria must be demonstrably work-related. Salary scales should be locally competitive so as to attract and retain highly-qualified individuals.

Screening procedures for applicants should be structured to eliminate people who are clearly unsuited -- psychologically, educationally, intellectually, physically, or morally -- to do police work. The agency will need to have minimum standards in these areas, including educational requirements, physical abilities, and character. Over 40 years ago, a national presidential commission recommended that all police have a minimum of a 4-year college degree. It is difficult to understand how any person with an educational level less than that could, today, perform the demanding and complex duties of a police officer in our society. But more important than eliminating unqualified applicants is identifying, through testing, medical and psychiatric examinations, personal interviews, and background investigations, the candidates with the necessary sensitivity, compassion, integrity, maturity, stability, and intelligence to handle the complexity, stress, and decision-making demanded of a police officer today.

The police agency should be representative of the community it serves. It should include proportionate numbers of racial and ethnic minorities, not only to correct past inequities, but also to demonstrate to minority communities that police authority is legitimate and inclusive. Women should be assigned to all field details according to their talents and skills. As to proportionate numbers of women, successful police agencies have numbers of women officers between 20 and 30 percent of the agency's strength. Research continues to show that women police are particularly effective at defusing violent situations and are less likely to use unnecessary force than male officers. Women and minority officers provide an essential and necessary balance within a police agency.

Those who are promoted to leadership positions within the agency must be selected on the basis of their practice of, and commitment to, the values of the agency, and not solely on their years of service. Coercive or abusive leadership styles have no place in a modern police agency.

Does the police agency provide high quality training for its officers?

Following selection of individuals to become police officers, the agency must train these individuals thoroughly and properly in all aspects of police work. They must be given guidance and skills to help them deal with all the problems and situations they will encounter in their work. They must be prepared to make quick and difficult decisions, to distinguish behavioral problems, to be knowledgeable about the different elements and cultures of the community, and to develop a range of effective conflict resolution skills including those necessary to have when dealing with the mentally ill.

The training curriculum should cover when and how to use force, when and when not to use firearms, criminal law and procedures, techniques for settling arguments, crime prevention and control, community relations and how to obtain citizens' cooperation, emergency care, and when and where to refer citizens for other community service resources; including the specifics of the agency's policy manual. Community social services, courts and correctional agencies should be studied and involved in the training to familiarize the officers with their operations and how they may be of assistance to the police and vice versa.

Recruits should be required to complete a physical fitness program and taught the importance of good health and fitness along with effective stress-reducing techniques. Additionally, they should be aware of the stress that police work puts on relationships and learn effective and healthy ways to deal with it. Recruits should spend time on the street, mentored by outstanding and specially prepared field training officers, doing hands-on police work. Monthly evaluation during an 18-24 month probationary period, should weed out those not meeting the standards and point to particular problems that need to be remedied before these officers are fully certified. At the end of the training period, all recruits should be required to pass a comprehensive examination to determine if they have mastered certain basic skills. Their knowledge of the Constitution, criminal law, the city and its various communities, and the agency's policy manual must be part of that examination.

A classroom and experiential training program such as described above would take at least six months to a year to administer properly. Although some states have minimum standards for police training, including time and subject areas, a wise police chief would make sure the training program was meeting the mission of the agency and be willing to supplement those areas not adequately addressed. That same chief would have a close relationship with training staff and make sure the atmosphere of the training academy is academic and consists of adult-based educational practices and that any stress placed on recruits was job-related. Swearing, cursing and other military-based "boot camp" styles of training should not be permitted.

Does the police agency reinforce the minimum requirements for a police officer serving in a free and democratic society?

Officers should receive a minimum level of training every year to keep them current on changes and new methods and developments within the police field and the social sciences. Annual training should reinforce and hold officers accountable for the four basic minimum requirements of a quality police officer:

- **Effectiveness**

Effectiveness is the ability of police officers to use the knowledge and skills they have been taught. Effective police work is work that gets the job done within the framework of legality and civility.

- **Integrity**

Those who are charged with enforcing our laws and maintaining order and security in our communities must be ethically sound. The nature of police work, its authority and use of power (including deadly force), its exposure to vice operations and large sums of money and/or illegal drugs, presents unique temptations. These and other ethical challenges arise in the course of any officer's workday. Officers must be able to resist these temptations if they are to enforce the laws fairly and consistently.

- **Civility and Courtesy**

The cornerstone upon which the police build trust and legitimacy within the community is through the on-going practice of civility and courtesy. Discourtesy and disrespect is the single most frequent complaint against police. Such behavior quickly erodes community trust and support for police. Trust and support, once lost, is extremely difficult to regain and, therefore, must be constantly maintained.

- **Health and physical fitness**

A balanced diet, moderate drinking habits, hobbies, sports, friendships with people who are not associated with police work, and routine physical exercise provide officers with the equilibrium necessary to perform their jobs well and a release from the physical and emotional stresses resulting from the nature of police work. Healthy police officers with good physical health and social outlets can maintain a proper perspective on their job and throughout their career.

Does the police agency guide, train, and supervise police officers in the restraint of the use of force?

Of all the decisions a police officer must make, that regarding the use of deadly force is the most difficult.

When police officers have to take a life it should be understood that it is a loss that impacts most everyone – the victim and his or her family, the officer doing the shooting, those who were in the immediate vicinity, and the entire community as well. Police must see themselves as primarily in the business of protecting and preserving life. The decision to use deadly force is often made instantaneously under conditions of extreme stress. The power to use non-negotiable force is a form of public trust given to the police and must be carefully used. The police agency, therefore, is responsible to the community for when and how its officers use force in carrying out their duties. Agencies should have formal, written policies about the proper use of force that do more than reflect the requirements of state law. The policies should define the boundaries of acceptable use of force, insure that officers receive thorough and adequate training, and are properly supervised.

The written policy must limit the use of deadly force to situations of extreme danger, after all other measures have failed or been ruled out, to safeguard life. Specifically, the policy should forbid officers from using deadly force to stop a crime suspect who tries to run away from the scene of a crime unless he or she poses a life-threatening danger to others. This includes the risky business of high-speed motor vehicle pursuits. Further, the policy should forbid shooting into crowds, over the heads of crowds, or at unseen persons inside buildings, or the use of warning shots. It is also imperative when an officer uses deadly force that persons outside the officer's agency investigate the incident and that the investigatory process is transparent.

If an officer discharges his or her weapon on or off duty, he or she should be required to file a written report on the incident so that supervisors can determine whether the incident was proper and legal. All officers should periodically meet the agency's standards regarding how and when to use firearms and demonstrate proficiency in techniques of arrest and physical restraint.

The agency should limit the use of the police baton to areas of the body below a person's head and have other policies in place regarding the use of any other kind of weapon such as chemical sprays and electronic devices such as Tasers. The use of handcuffs or "flex cuffs" should also be addressed in written policies and training practices. Generally, restraining devices are permitted when an officer reasonably believes that a suspect may attempt to escape, or may pose a danger to himself or others. The agency should require officers to file a written report whenever they use force, including use of restraints, whether or not it causes an injury.

Is the police agency willing to investigate and discipline officers engaging in misconduct?

If a police agency is to have the trust of the community, it must establish clear standards of behavior for its officers, and it must handle citizen complaints swiftly and impartially. Officers must know, unequivocally, the standard to which they will be held accountable, and there must be accessible and thorough procedures for investigating citizen complaints, no matter the source -- anonymous tip, person under arrest, juvenile, or suspect awaiting trial -- and those procedures must be perceived as unbiased.

The agency should make information available regarding how to make a complaint against an officer or procedure of the agency on its website and have written brochures available for the public. It should describe the various steps in the process and a copy given to every citizen who files a complaint. This form should include the name, email address, and telephone number of the person handling the investigation.

It is extremely important that the citizen complaint system be designed to safeguard the due process rights of both citizens and police officers and include the right to consult an attorney, to have an attorney or advocate present during the process, and to be protected from any intimidation or threats. The agency should also see to it that all complaint investigations are completed within 30 days and that citizens are regularly kept informed of the status of their complaints. When a complaint investigation has been completed and a decision made, the police chief should inform the complainant by letter of the decision and of appeal procedures to use if he or she is not satisfied with the decision. Guilty officers should be disciplined in a manner that reflects the seriousness of the misconduct, the extent of wrongdoing or injury to the victim, and the officer's service record and history of prior complaints.

It is critically important that all officers know that the agency will not tolerate illegal or improper conduct, and that it views prevention as its first line of defense. To this end, the agency must choose only the best applicants; provide written guides to proper conduct; give adequate training and supervision to officers; make available stress reduction and employee assistance programs; and keep in constant touch with citizens' concerns and problems through regular communication with community leaders. If these preventative measures fail for some officers, a system of early identification should be created to identify officers in need of re-training, monitoring, or special help. If these remedial measures fail for errant officers, dismissal must be strongly considered.

5

ORGANIZATIONAL CHARACTERISTICS

Do police officers respect individual rights?

The most important responsibility of police officers is to protect citizens' civil rights. They are the foundation of our society and our rule of law. The most critical aspect of this respect for law is in a police officer's willingness to abide strictly by the legal requirements for arrest, the use of force, searches and seizures of persons and property, and in stop and frisk situations. Such willingness is grounded in the officer's understanding that the ends do not justify the means in policing, that they cannot break the law in order to enforce it. Nor can they succumb to community pressures to violate suspect's rights in order to solve a crime or to abuse citizens' rights to freedom of assembly to solve a public nuisance problem. While this fundamental principle of insuring due process may make the job of controlling crime and preventing disorder more difficult, it is, without exception, the hallmark of a professional police officer. These important values work best when they are internalized into every aspect of police work throughout an officer's career.

Respect for law is particularly important when an officer takes a person into custody. The agency must expect and demand that an arresting officer is responsible for the physical safety of a person in custody until that custody is officially turned over to another legally responsible person. Officers must comply with all court-directed or advised procedures, such as reading to all suspects, including juveniles, the Miranda warning against self-incrimination before interrogating them. Arresting officers should make sure persons in custody understand the reason for the arrest and what actions are likely to be taken against them. Further, the agency must allow arrested persons to notify relatives and confer with an attorney promptly after the arrest. Any questioning of the arrested person must be conducted within legal requirements and in a non-abusive manner.

In the area of freedom of speech and assembly, the police agency should provide for the safety of public protestors regardless of their political beliefs. Officers should be assigned to protect them from any acts of violence.

Officers have a particular responsibility to abide by the legal requirements for information-gathering and surveillance. This is especially important today with the advent of drones and other electronic methods of gathering information. Any intrusion into a person's private conversations, correspondence (including that which is communicated electronically) should be covered by a warrant, and no information gathered as a result of such intrusions or data-gathering should ever be used to harass, intimidate, blackmail, or publicly humiliate a person.

Does the police agency address crime and order problems by using all community resources?

The traditional police response to these problems has been either to focus on solving each individual case or to increase routine patrol or investigative operations. These responses have not notably been successful, most probably because they are reactions to crises or to public pressure rather than well-conceived problem-solving operations. A good police agency will be striving to put in place a comprehensive program of crime deterrence based on a thorough knowledge of the nature and extent of the problem: where it occurs, when it occurs, who is most often the victim, and who appears to be causing it. Solving the problem should involve both police measures as well as those of other governmental agencies, social services, and resources from the affected community. It is especially important that police resist the temptation to ease public pressure, particularly following a sensational crime, or persistent community problems with popular, yet knowingly ineffective, strategies.

The police are an integral part of the total community's response to a problem, They should not be separate and distinct from other service agencies in the community which can help solve the problem. A skillful police chief will coordinate and involve other service agencies to solve community problems such as public inebriates, homeless people, or the lack of recreational and social facilities for young people. The police should not succumb to the notion that all community problems, *per se*, are their responsibility. They should always attempt to work with other service agencies. The handling of mentally ill persons is one example of a problem for which the police should coordinate their efforts and team with community mental health workers. Housing shelters, detox centers and other medical facilities provide for the physical safety of those who are most vulnerable in our society and much preferred to the use of the jail. The responses to drug abuse, family violence, and juvenile delinquency, although they have a law enforcement dimension, should always involve public welfare and mental health service agencies in the community, A wise police chief looks at failures in systems which cause crime and disorder with the community and then teams with educators, business leaders, probation and parole officers, and elected officials in finding solutions.

In this respect, police must recognize that they are the primary case finders, and often first-responders, for many of these outside agencies, as well as gatekeepers to the criminal justice system. Officers must be equipped with the skills to diagnose individuals' immediate problems and be aware of, and able to refer them, to available community services. Since much of police work is not related to solving crime, but to helping those who are too young or too old, too poor or too ill to care for themselves, it is important that officers know how to provide special and compassionate care for these citizens and to whom they should be referred.

These creative responses must also be applied to other community problems that pose a public nuisance, such as noise complaints, dogs at large, speeding cars, and teenage loitering. Officers must be trained to work with neighborhood groups to reach a voluntary solution, if possible, among those most directly affected by the problem and to be able to enlist their input and help in its solution. Such efforts require the development of mediation and negotiation skills among officers and their leaders.

Does the police agency cooperate and coordinate with neighboring law enforcement agencies and other agencies in the criminal justice system?

A good way for police to reduce their costs and increase their effectiveness is to pool their resources with those of neighboring agencies. Working together, they can engage in cooperative purchasing agreements, data collection and record keeping services, training programs, communications networks, recruitment and selection activities, crime analysis, and laboratory facilities. The exchange of personnel and sharing skills can contribute to job growth and development. It can be particularly helpful if, for example, an individual officer's combination of skill and experience is needed to solve a complex crime in another agency, conduct a training program, or provide foreign language translations. Many agencies regularly participate in county or area-wide task forces to work on specific cases or problems such as organized crime, burglary rings, criminal gangs, drug cartels, other criminal enterprises, or to assist various state or federal law enforcement agencies with their mission.

Police agencies should maintain open lines of communication with the prosecutor's office, courts, probation, and correctional agencies in addressing community crime problems. One action or policy change in one of these agencies invariably affects the others. The agencies' leaders should participate in a formal coordinating council that meets regularly to discuss mutual problems, share information, and improve on what they do.

Does the police agency communicate with the public?

Ideally, there should be a free and easy exchange between the police agency and the community, which includes its news media. If media personnel perceive that agency leaders are accessible to them, that their questions will be promptly and accurately answered, that their opinions about agency practices are respected, they are more likely to regard the police with respect and trust and share that regard with the public.

The responsibility for establishing this atmosphere of openness and trust rests with the chief, and it must be internally present within the agency. The chief should schedule regular meetings with groups of officers and their union officials to explore new ideas, listen to ways to improve work, and discuss grievances. Officers from all ranks should be involved in developing major policies in the agency, and the chief should work closely with them to insure the success of any changes. In a modern police agency, leaders need to know and understand the work that officers do and the relationship they have with the community.

Taking this effort to a broader dimension, the chief must possess a personal style that is open, collaborative, honest, and involves community leaders in policy deliberations, Many successful chiefs have established citizen advisory councils at the neighborhood level that alert the police to developing problems, air citizens' grievances, and develop plans for cooperative crime prevention or disorder reduction ventures. These advisory councils also serve as a valuable forum for the police to explain why they do, why they have taken certain actions or instituted certain policies and practices, or to mediate clashes between the public and police and negotiate a solution, or how they have successful responded to a problem. A wise police chief can use these meetings to educate the citizens about serious crime problems -- drug-related deaths among young people, for example -- and cite the reasons for what may have been an unpopular police action, such as making drug-related arrests at a high school. At the same time, the chief must acknowledge the community's legitimate concern about various police practices and see this as an opportunity to explain, listen, or to make needed changes.

Although the chief leads the way and sets the tone for openness and candor with the community, this tone must pervade the agency. Officers should be expected to incorporate close community relations as an essential part of their work, not a burden or waste of time. Officers can and should speak to community groups, neighborhood associations, school assemblies, and meetings of business and social clubs; they should conduct public education programs such as bicycle safety, theft prevention, and home security; conduct programs in which citizens ride or walk along with police and observe them at work. Officers should be encouraged and given time to meet with community leaders and neighborhood representatives. They should make an effort during the course of their regular duties to talk to people about police policies and to establish strong working relationships with a wide range of people on their beats.

How does the police agency approach the news media?

Although news media relations are particularly sensitive, agency leaders must recognize that the media, and all its current permutations on the Internet, including social media, the audio and video capabilities of smart phones, and government and corporate video cameras in the marketplace, have changed how the public gets its information. These media can be a valuable way to reach the largest possible number of people with information about agency policies, practices, and viewpoints on matters of public interest. Today, the term "news media" is used in the broadest sense. An active news media are necessary watchdogs over government and its activities. It can be said today that everyone with a smart phone is a news photographer and reporter. One has only to search police related incidents on YouTube to make this point. While this situation may be difficult for police to accept, it is a fact. Therefore, an open and positive attitude toward every citizen is essential for open discussion, exchange of ideas, and explanation of police practices. These new media can be a valuable ally for a chief trying to find solutions to complex problems, inform the public of the police function, ask for help, and move the agency toward more openness and better accountability.

To this end, police leaders should be available to answer inquiries from every citizen, and officers should have guidance about what they are allowed to disclose. Furthermore, the agency should generate public interest stories by, for example, issuing a news release about a new police practice and what the agency hopes it will accomplish, holding a face-to-face media conferences to discuss a pressing problem, or, as some agencies have recently done, post examples of police helping citizens, saving lives, helping people in trouble, or other positive agency actions using various social media sites like Facebook. An agency that only reacts to incidents or events or that disperses information only in response to a reporter's inquiries will be perceived as closed and secretive.

At the same time, the agency should work with media representatives to develop policies about the nature and scope of information to be released in a sensational case such as a hostage situation, kidnapping, or a domestic terrorism incident. These policies should balance the public's right to know, the media's need for immediate information, and when that information can be released. The purpose of such a policy is not to censor or control the news media, but to secure the cooperation of the media, avoid misunderstandings during tense and stressful situations, the respect the needs of agency investigators.

We should now be aware of the kinds of questions we should ask our police. The answers to the following will identify some of the most important functions and characteristics of a modern and effective police agency.

But evaluating and rating the characteristics of the leadership, organization, and policies of a police agency is only a means toward an end. As citizens, we should be primarily concerned with the quality of our local police service: how well are our police fulfilling their triple obligation to control crime, maintain order, and provide service and garnering our trust while they do it?

Good leadership, sound organization, and well-conceived policies are the building blocks of a high quality police agency. It is both our right and our obligation as citizens to inquire of our police agency, ask questions, and decide for ourselves if everyone who resides in, or visits our community, has their public safety needs met.

To assist us in this inquiry, the check list on the following section is provided.

6

THE CHECKLIST

RATING YOUR LOCAL POLICE

A. Leadership Characteristics

1. What kind of person is the chief?

- Does he/she have a clear vision?   __Yes __No __Unknown

- Does everyone know that vision? __Yes __No __Unknown

- Is the chief's leadership style collaborative and respectful? (See *Principles of Quality Leadership on p. 53.*)   __Yes __No __Unknown

- Does the chief have a willingness to challenge the *status quo*?   __Yes __No __Unknown

- Does the chief take risks, be innovative, and build a coalition of support for change?   __Yes __No __Unknown

- Does the chief portray self-confidence with humility?   __Yes __No __Unknown

- Does the chief have a track record of personal integrity?   Yes No Unknown

- Does he/she have the respect of community and elected officials?   Yes No __Unknown

- Does the chief inspire and motivate?   __Yes __No __Unknown

2. What tone does the chief set for the agency?

- Does he/she have a coherent and concrete crime control strategy?   Yes No Unknown

- Does it include crime prevention?   __Yes No __Unknown

- Does the chief defend the rights of unpopular groups?   Yes No Unknown

- Does he/she see that police services are delivered equally and fairly to the community?   Yes __No __Unknown

- Are organizational decisions based on data and not emotions?   __Yes __No __Unknown

3. Does the chief articulate the policies of the agency clearly and understandably?

- Does the chief speak out and take stands? __Yes __No __Unknown

- Is he/she an articulate a spokesperson on crime control and public safety?   Yes No __Unknown

- Does the chief advise the community on personal security?   __Yes __No __Unknown

- Does he/she seek to preserve guarantees of due process?   __Yes __No __Unknown

- Does the chief stand up and defend minority rights?   __Yes __No __Unknown

- Does he/she assure protection for the weak and injured?   Yes No Unknown

- Is the chief an able manager in the complex bureaucracy of policing?   __Yes __No __Unknown

- Does the chief act as a guardian of the rule of law?   __Yes __No __Unknown

B. Policy Characteristics

Does the police agency have a clear sense of its objectives?

- Are there written policies for all operational practices?   __Yes __No __Unknown

- Does the police agency select the finest individuals to be police officers?   Yes No __Unknown

- Are officers promoted on the basis of ability and practice of organizational values and not solely seniority?   __Yes __No __Unknown

- Does the agency provide high quality training for its officers in an adult learning style without harassment?   __Yes __No __Unknown

- Does the agency reinforce the minimum requirements for a good police officer: effectiveness, integrity, civility and courtesy, and physical fitness?   __Yes __No __Unknown

- Does the agency guide, train, and supervise police officers in the proper use of physical force? __Yes __No __Unknown

- Is the agency committed to preserving human life and treating all people with dignity and respect? __Yes __No __Unknown

- Is the police agency willing to investigate and discipline its employees who engage in misconduct?   __Yes __No __Unknown

- When things go wrong, does the agency look to improve systems or blame people? __Yes __No __Unknown

C. Organizational Characteristics

- Do police officers in the agency respect individual rights?   __Yes __No __Unknown

- Does the police agency address crime and order problems by using all community resources?
  __Yes __No __Unknown

- Are they willing to collaborate and work with outside agencies in furtherance of their goals?
  __Yes __No __Unknown

- Does the agency specifically cooperate and coordinate with neighboring law enforcement agencies and other agencies in the enforcement, prevention, and treatment systems?
  __Yes __No __Unknown

- Does the agency communicate well with the public?   __Yes __No __Unknown

- Is the agency open to inquiries from the news media?   __Yes __No __Unknown

- Is the agency accountable and reasonably transparent?   Yes No Unknown

These are important questions we need to ask and for which police leaders need to clearly and satisfactorily respond.

The bottom line is this: we should expect and demand that our police officers hold a college degree, be carefully selected, well-trained, and controlled in their use of force, honest in their actions, including reports and court testimony, courteous to every person regardless of their station in life, led by mature leaders, and closely in touch with us.

Police leaders should also model these characteristics and be highly mature, good listeners, and willing to work closely with their officers and members of the community.

7

POSTSCRIPT

Now that we are familiar with the characteristics of a high quality police agency, we may want to explore ways to improve our local police agency. In this postscript, we can find one of the earliest descriptions of how to police a democracy. It comes from London in the 1820s and is as pertinent today as it was over 150 years ago.

We can also find a recent excerpt on "Qualities of Police in a Free and Democratic Society." It describes the working qualities which police must hold and practice in a free and democratic society.

Next are three short descriptions of what quality policing, community-oriented policing, and quality leadership "is" against what it "is not." They will help us form further evaluative questions regarding our police agency.

- Is our police agency a high-quality organization?
- Do our police practice community-oriented policing?
- Do police leaders practice the "new leadership?"

Early Principles of Policing

1.   Police exist to prevent crime and disorder.

2.   Police ability to perform their duties is dependent upon public approval of police actions.

3.   Police must secure the willing co-operation of the public in obeying the law to be able to secure and maintain the public's respect.

4.   Police ability to secure public co-operation diminishes the need to use physical force.

5.   Police preserve public support not by catering to public opinion but by demonstrating impartial service to the law.

6.   Police use physical force to enforce the law or restore order only when persuasion, advice and warning is insufficient.

7.   Police and the public share policing responsibilities.

8.   Police should never appear to take on the powers of the judiciary.

9.   Police effectiveness is to be measured by the absence of crime and disorder, not the visible evidence of police action in dealing with it.[6]

---

[6] "Principles of Policing." Sir Robert Peel, Richard Mayne, and Charles Rowan. London, circa 1830.

QUALITIES OF POLICE IN A FREE AND DEMOCRATIC SOCIETY
(Abridged)

David C. Couper and Michael S. Scott

We believe the following qualities of democratic policing set forth a template that police as well as citizens and their elected representatives can use to evaluate the police institution and, if found wanting, use to guide the quest for continuous improvement.

This statement of principles is not intended to be critical of our nation's police but rather to help all of us clarify the nature of our function, public expectations, and the central importance of the police role in a society that professes to pursue justice fairly, equally, and without bias.

Qualities of Police in a Free and Democratic Society

1. Accountable. Police recognize the nature and extent of their discretionary authority and must always be accountable to the people, their elected representatives, and the law for their actions, and be as transparent as possible in their decision-making.

2. **Collaborative.** Police must be able to collaborate, as appropriate, with community members and other organizations in settling disagreements, choosing policing strategies, and solving policing problems. This collaborative style must also apply to the way police departments are led and managed. This means police leaders must actively listen to their officers and work with them in identifying and resolving department and community problems.

3. Educated and trained. All police officers with arrest powers should begin their career with a broad and advanced education in the sciences and humanities. Training should consist of rigorous and extensive training courses in an adult-learning climate that teaches both the ethics and skills of democratic policing.

4. Effective and preventive. The mark of a good police department and the officers who work within it is that they continuously seek to handle their business more effectively and fairly, emphasizing preventing crime and disorder and not merely responding to it, and applying research and practical knowledge, using problem-solving methods, toward that end.

5. Honest. Honesty and good ethical practice are essential. The search for and cultivation of these traits begin with the selection process and continue throughout an officer's career. Only those police candidates who have demonstrated good decision-making so far in their lives should be selected.

6. Model citizen. Police officers must not only be good police officers, but good citizens as well, modeling the values and virtues of good citizenship in their professional and personal lives.

7. Peacekeeper and protector. The police role is, above all else, that of community peacekeepers, and not merely law enforcers or crime fighters. Their training, work, and values all point towards the keeping of peace in the community. As gatekeepers to the criminal justice system, police must see themselves as defenders and protectors of Constitutional and human rights, especially for those who cannot defend or care for themselves in our society.

8. Representative. The members of police organizations must be demographically representative of the communities they serve, both because it reflects fair employment opportunities and because it enables the police to be more effective in achieving their objectives.

9. Respectful. Police officers should treat all persons with unconditional courtesy and respect, and be willing to listen to others, especially to those without social power or status. Likewise, police leaders should treat their workers with courtesy and respect their employment rights.

10. Restrained. The preservation of life should be the foundation for all police use of force. Police officers should continually prepare themselves to use physical force in a restrained and proper manner, with special training in its application to those who are mentally ill. Deadly force should be used only as a last resort and only when death or serious injury of the officer or another person is imminent. Less-than-lethal force should be preferred where possible.

11. Servant leader. Every police officer, regardless of rank, must simultaneously be a good leader and a good servant, to the public and to the police organization. Servant leaders use their authority and influence to improve others' welfare.

12. Unbiased. Although some bias is inherent in human nature, police officers recognize that they can and should train themselves to reduce their biases and deal with all people fairly and without regard to their race, ethnicity, gender, socio-economic condition, national origin, citizenship status, or sexual orientation.

A HIGH-QUALITY POLICE AGENCY

IS	IS NOT
Focused on serving others.	Them versus us.
Community collaborative.	Emotionally disengaged.
Lawful/honest in practice.	Corrupt and self-serving.
Values formal education.	Anti-education.
Solves community problems.	Responds to incidents.
Respectful to everyone.	Discourteous.
Driven by society's values.	Driven by subcultural values.
Protects and guards.	Military warrior.
Helpful and compassionate.	Uncaring and unfeeling.
Considers policing a noble calling.	Considers policing merely a job.

COMMUNITY-ORIENTED POLICING

IS	IS NOT
Collaborative guardians.	Dominating warriors.
Close to people.	Centralized.
Citizen-identified problems.	Concerned with police problems.
Broad problem-solving.	Focused on incidents.
Geographical responsibility.	Time of day responsibility.
Supporting societal values.	Reinforcing subcultural values.
Increasing the quality of life.	About statistics and numbers.
Compassionate.	Just the facts.
Way of doing business.	One of many programs.
Empowering, coaching leaders.	Top-down, coercive leaders.
Continuous improvement.	Maintains the *status quo*.

THE NEW LEADERSHIP

IS	IS NOT
Systems thinking.	Event thinking.
Data-based decisions.	Decisions by emotion.
Customer-oriented.	Self-oriented.
Teamwork.	Individual work
Empowering others.	Limiting others.
Coaching.	Dictating.
Respecting others.	Coercive/demeaning.
Continuous improvement.	Maintaining *status quo*.
Growing others.	Controlling others.

PRINCIPLES OF QUALITY
LEADERSHIP

1. Believe in, foster, and support teamwork.

2. Be committed to the problem-solving process; use it and let data, not emotions, drive decisions.

3. Seek employees input before you make key decisions.

4. Believe that the most effective way to improve the quality of work or service is to ask and listen to employees who are doing the work.

5. Strive to develop mutual respect and trust among employees; drive out fear.

6. Have a customer orientation and focus toward employees and citizens.

7. Manage according to the behavior of 95 percent of employees and not the 5 percent who cause problems. Deal with the 5 percent promptly and fairly.

8. Improve systems and examine processes before blaming people.

9. Avoid "top-down," power-oriented decision- making whenever possible.

10. Encourage creativity through risk-taking and be tolerant of honest mistakes.

11. Be a facilitator and coach. Develop an open atmosphere that encourages providing and accepting feedback.

12. With teamwork, develop with employees agreed-upon goals and a plan to achieve them. *[Couper, circa 1985]*

EIGHT PILLARS OF
POLICING A FREE SOCIETY

1. Policing is a necessary function; a noble and learned calling.
2. Only those who represent society's highest values should serve as police.
3. Policing is more than enforcing the law; it is serving people, being present, solving problems, and helping others.
4. The nature of policing requires those who practice it be highly respectful, compassionate, and collaborative in carrying out their duties.
5. The use of legitimate force is a public trust given to police to be used wisely and carefully.
6. Those who practice policing must be impeccably honest.
7. Police must have respect and tolerance for dissent and public protest.
8. Ultimately, police are guardians of our way of life, to be accountable and transparent in their actions, and protectors of our Bill of Rights and persons most vulnerable in society. *[Couper, 2015]*

ABOUT THE AUTHOR

David C. Couper was chief of police in Madison, Wisc. when he wrote the first edition of this publication in 1983. He served as Madison's chief of police for over 20 years from 1972 to 1993. He entered as a police officer with the Edina, Minn., department in 1960. He then joined the Minneapolis Police Department where he served as a patrol officer, training officer, and detective. In 1968, Couper was appointed director of public safety for Burnsville, a suburb of Minneapolis. In 1972, he was called to be chief of police in Madison, Wisc. He received undergraduate and graduate degrees from the University of Minnesota. Over his 25 years as a police chief, he developed particular expertise in the areas of handling public protest, mass demonstrations, conflict management, and transformational leadership. Since his retirement, he attended seminary at Nashotah House, received another graduate degree, and was ordained as a priest in the Episcopal Church. Since that time, he has served parishes in Portage and North Lake, Wisc. and maintains his passion for policing on the weblog "Improving Police" which can be found on Wordpress.com. He and his wife, Sabine Lobitz, a retired State Capitol police captain, live on their woodland property west of Madison near the Blue Mounds.

Other books by David Couper:

- *Quality Policing: The Madison Experience* (1991)

- *Arrested Development: A Veteran Police Chief Sounds Off About Protest, Racism, Corruption and the Seven Steps Necessary to Improve Our Nation's Police* (2012)

- *The New Quality Leadership Workbook* (2014)

These books may be purchased at CreateSpace.com, Amazon.com, or from your local bookstore.

www.ingramcontent.com/pod-product-compliance
Lightning Source LLC
Chambersburg PA
CBHW071119280526

45787CB00003B/1095